· MEET ·
EDGAR DEGAS

Read with You Center for
Excellence in STEAM Education

Read With You

Published by Read With You Publishing. Printed in the United States of America.
Read With You and associated logos are trademarks and/or registered trademarks of Read With You L.L.C.
ISBN: 979-8-88618-083-1
First Edition January 2022

Self-Portrait with White Collar, c. 1857

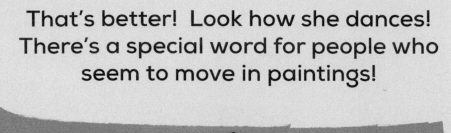

The Rehearsal Onstage, c. 1874

Dancers, Pink and Green, c. 1890

Dancers Practicing at the Barre, 1877

Woman Viewed from Behind (Visit to a Museum), c. 1879–1885

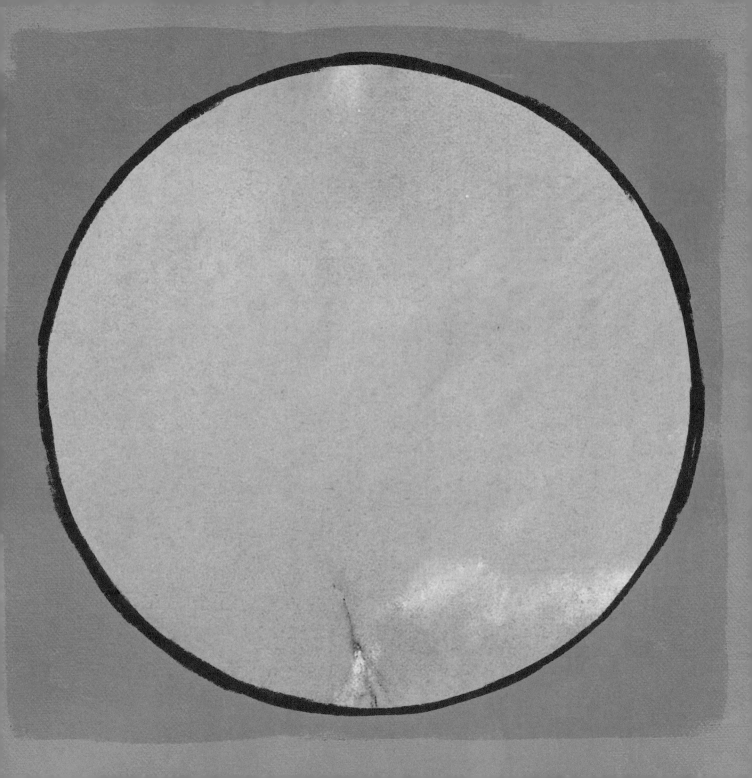

Beach at Low Tide (Mouth of the River), 1869

The Star, 1879–1881

Dancer in Green, c. 1883

Find Examples

This painting is *The Dance Class* (1874). It shows people doing many things!

What are some of the gestures you can spot?

Who looks like they are moving the most?

Who looks like they are not moving?

Connect

Degas also made statues, like this one titled *Little Dancer Aged Fourteen*, 1878-1881.

Can you copy the dancer's position?

Look through the book. Which other dancers cross their legs like her?

She was made with wax and dressed in clothes made from real cloth. What would it feel like to touch her?

Craft

Option 1

1. Ask an adult for tracing paper and a pen or pencil.

2. Put the tracing paper over a few of the dancers in the paintings in this book and use a pen or pencil to trace their shapes.

3. Which shapes do you like most? Why?

Option 2

1. Pick your favorite kind of dance!

2. Take a photo of yourself or someone else dancing.

3. Looking at the photo, draw a picture of the dancer. How can you show that they are moving?

Made in the USA
Coppell, TX
20 July 2023

19385356R00024